DANK HOUSE MANOR PUBLISHING

iDRIP

By

Neil S. Reddy

An existential farce of angst, food poisoning and revenge.

Published by Dank House Manor Publishing 2016

Dankhousemanorpublishing.com

dankhousemanorpublishing@gmail.com

For

Di

With gratitude to L.

iDRIP

An existential farce of angst, food poisoning and revenge.

Outline

To be played as a farce with sinister overtones.

Please regard the entirety of this script - including dialogue, staging suggestions, music and numbers of cast members - as completely and utterly adaptable, subject to change due to circumstance and funding limitations. The script as it is set-out here should be regarded as guidelines not gospel, written for theatre not stone.

Raymond Ekal, a voice in someone's head tells his comic, tragic tale of becoming 'a voice in someone's head.'

Raymond is a man who turned to drink and then turned into a drink. His life fell apart and then he felt apart, becoming a glass of water…but then redemption presents itself in the form of revenge.

The characters and players within the piece are Raymond's remembrance of them – they, and he, are all 'in the head,' this is his tale, his vengeance and therefore he can tell it any way he likes – this provides the production with many options, angles and opportunities to playout Ekal's story.

For this reason all set pieces, such as fantasy scenes, dreams and imaginings are open to adlib and alteration.

Characters

Raymond Ekal

Raymond Ekal – an unemployed drug rep, music lover and fulltime drinker whom fate chooses to toy with and make a better and yet lesser man. He is also a voice in someone else's head. He talks directly to the head / audience as he interacts with the cast.

Wendy

Raymond's long suffering life partner, she is on the edge of walking away from her inconsiderate fool of a boyfriend. Wendy is a decent human being in a difficult situation – she has found love elsewhere and her guilt is eating her up – until Ekal lets her down once too often.

Beryl

Aging club owner and heavy drinker, heavy smoker, loud mouth who, from time to time, takes mercy on fellow travellers who are down on their luck. Raymond describes her as a mix of Marianne Faithful, Humphrey Bogart and Quasimodo –

always wears a claret coloured beret, and yes she does have a bit of a hunchback.

Pete

Trim, buff and possibly the coolest barman in the world, he can end a bar fight with a stern (and somewhat twisted phrase.)

Dr Caz

A young female A&E doctor – who lacks any bedside manner.

Maurice

According to Beryl, Maurice is the clubs official "pontificating ponce," which he takes as a compliment.

Big Bob

Beryl's sinister brother. A London gangster with a heart of limes.

Minor Characters / The Busy People

These can played by members of the main cast - given there are a minimum of six players – or a separate non speaking chorus line. There are four speaking parts.

Sandwich Board Man /Chorus– enacting the 'talk-over' sequences.

Police Inspector and Police Officer.

Rugger and Hugger – Aussie rugby fans.

Boss and Secretary

Barman /Coffee shop guy / Fireman/ Muggers

Wendy's new fella.

Guitar / bass player

Female blues singer / Female nurse.

iDRIP

by

Neil S. Reddy.

*Opening scene – stage in darkness – a small blue
lights flickers above the stage as Raymond begins
to speak as synapses are flashing into life. Stage
slowly brightens.*

Raymond

(Centre stage – unseen in the dark)

Do you hear this thought? Yes you do. A miracle!
Yes a thought, an echo between your synapses. A
voice that is not your own, talking aloud within.

Is that a cold sweat I feel? Yeah you can hear me.
Calm down, sit down and shut up. I'm not going to
hurt you.

No, you're not crazy, I am in your head. I'm in
your head.

Listen, of course I have a story to tell you. I want
to explain how I came to be stuck in your head,
really it's the only decent thing to do…shhh…
would it help if I illustrated the tale, do you need a
diagram, a comic book explanation? Okay then…

(Stage lights on – we see the club, it's a tatty bar, with tables and a miss match of chairs .A mural made up of posters of jazz and blues singers, covers the far wall.) Raymond is crouched into a ball his forehead on the floor centre stage, he's wearing a washed out overly large dressing gown.)

Raymond

Hello…so here I am…wow yeah here I am, and pretty close too, but I see myself as taller or did, anyhow we'll come back to that… so an explanation is in order, how did I get in here… where to begin… the job interview?

(Raymond takes off dressing gown - he has a suit on underneath – he sits down – a secretary sits stage left reading a magazine – Raymond gives her a nod and a wink, he's trying it on.)

Raymond

Unemployed but earnest; that was me. I'd been a drug rep, all legal stuff! Nothing dodgy, apart from the entire concept of selling wellbeing in a pill. I think it was my lack of conviction in the products that lost me the last job.

(Enter Wendy stage right.)

Wendy

That and being pissed as a fart during a
presentation!

Raymond

Ah, this is Wendy... the voice of reason and...

Wendy

Get a job Ray! Get a job! I can't carry us both, it's
not fair. It's not fair!

Raymond

Unrelenting reality. Don't worry babe I've got it
covered. I've got a new Powerpoint presentation,
lovely new crisp hand-outs and I've been
researching their product for days, and... I'm as
sober as toilet water, don't worry.

Wendy

Don't worry... don't worry. All I do is worry Ray.
Worry and provide for you and clean up after you
and make excuses for... we need this... we need
this job...I'll see you later. (Storms off muttering)

Raymond

Now don't be too hard on her, she has a lot to put up with…me… But really, this time, short of an act of God or insider dealing, the job's mine.

Boss

(Enters stage left) Mr Ekal, Raymond Ekal? I'm afraid there's been a communications breakdown. The post was filled two weeks ago. We thought you'd been informed. Never mind, better luck next time. (Exit Boss and secretary – with a sniff - stage left)

Raymond

Bastard. As quick as that… he didn't even apologise. He didn't offer to pay my bus fare either… gutted and out of pocket… oh well you know what they say: when life serves you lemons, kick the bastard in the throat…or make a whiskey sour.

(Raymond moves to the bar – the Barman appears and Raymond is joined at the bar by two large rugby players – Rugger and Hook.)

Raymond

Whiskey please, large one with a large one.

Barman

Which one?

Raymond

The nearest....

Rugger

Blah Blah Blah Blah

Hook

Blah Blah Blah Blah

Raymond

Oh they were talking sport or something equally pointless and I really wasn't interested, they're only here because of what happens next...

Barman

Rough day guvnor?

Raymond

Guvnor? Don't you just hate that? Do I look like a
governor?

(To barman) You could say that, but nothing Mr
Bells can't put right...

Barman

(Places glass on bar) That's a shame, because
that's Teachers.

Raymond

Whatever... bottoms up?   *(Raymond places
glass to his lips totters, drops glass and collapses)*

Rugger

(Suddenly developing bad Aussie accent)

Strewth! Hooky! The limeys done a flat liner!

Hook

Strewth! 32 to 2 Rugger! I'll do the kissing.
(Southern 'Deliverance' accent) Cause he sure got
a purrty mouth.

*(Rugger and Hook (feel free to adlib) start very
energetic CPR – loud counting with lots of added
shouts of encouragement to each other and
Raymond – which Raymond talks through)*

Raymond

To be honest, I'm not sure they were Aussies or
perverts or that they could count, but I know they
saved my life and... ow... easy there! They also
broke three of my ribs. Of course I don't remember
any of this but I do remember my dream.

*(Rugger and Hook – start acting like Kangaroos –
and jumping around the stage.)*

Rugger & Hook

Water my whiskey down blue, water my whiskey
down... (Repeat till exit)

Raymond (Standing)

It was pretty weird.

Hook (Enter)

Water, water… but not a drop to drip, drip, drip.
(Exit)

Raymond

Bloody weird.   The next thing I knew I was in
hospital.

*(Four doctors/ nurses in white coats + Sister in
blue; rush onto the stage with a 'trolley/ bed'
which they throw Raymond onto and a 'medical
monitor' – they all freeze look at Raymond and
shout.)*

He's Alive!

(All exit – except Sister & Dr Caz)

Raymond *(sits up)*

Okay they probably didn't say that either, but how
cool would that have been? No, the next thing I
remember is this teenage girl lurking around my
bed…and the machine next to me was going crazy.

(Sound – high pitch monitor alarm)

Dr Caz

Bloody machine…

Sister

Shut the alarm off!

Dr Caz

I have, three times. But it thinks he's dead.

Sister

Well is he?

Raymond

I'm fine

Sister

So turn it off!

Dr Caz

But it says he's dead…

Sister

So it's knackered…give it here, I'll take it to the elderly ward. *(Exit with monitor)*

Raymond

So will I live or not?

Dr Caz

Not for much longer if you keep drinking like that…

Raymond

Drinking like what? I didn't have a…

Dr Caz

Your blood alcohol level came in at 520… that's very nearly a cocktail. People usually die with that level of alcohol in their system.

Raymond

Doctor, I didn't have a drop. I ordered a large one true but…

Dr Caz

Blood results don't lie! Denial is not going to solve the problem! *(Exit)*

Raymond

Well that told me didn't it... did I drink that whiskey?

Dr Caz *(Enters and exits)*

Blood results don't lie! Get some therapy!

Raymond

And to quote John Lee Hooker... out the door I went.

(Nurse enters – pushes him off trolley and exits). Of course the sensible thing to do would have been to phone Wendy...but I wasn't feeling that brave... I needed a bolt hole and some... encouragement... the Dutch kind.

(Enter double bass player – plays slow walking blues rift – Bb.)

Raymond

Live music…I love it, any colour, any creed any flavour. This is Beryl's place, not the clubs real name but we all call it that, Beryl's Club. Live music six nights a week, it's not much to look at… not unlike Beryl actually…

(Beryl enters with a hacking cough – she sits on a barstool at the end of the bar surveying her domain – she leers at audience, lights a cigarette and nods to the bass man.)

Raymond

That's Beryl… what a woman, a rare mix of Marianne Faithful, Humphrey Bogart and Quasimodo.

Beryl

Can he fucking play or what?

Raymond

All class.

Beryl

Ray, you tosser, aint seen you in weeks!

Raymond

I was here last night Beryl.

Beryl

Really? Well, you look like shit.

Raymond

Real class.... You've heard of the diamond in the rough...that's the rough.

Beryl *(Coughs and then spits)*

Jesus! That one looks like Buddha!

Raymond

Classy...

Maurice *(Enter – very camp OTT)*

Raymond… exquisitely turned out as ever I see. You must tell me the name of your tailor… I know people.

Raymond

Maurice… is Maurice.

Maurice

Beryl darling… *(Kiss kiss)*

Beryl

Ponce.

Maurice

Charming. Peter, Malibu and coke darling.

Beryl

So Ray, are you drinking or playing with your dick? Pete, get this wanker a drink. Pete!

Pete

I heard you Beryl...

Raymond

Pete the barman... very cool guy. The kind of guy that should have his own theme music. The kind of guy, guys like me want to be!

Pete

Large one with a large one, right Ray?

Raymond

So cool! I once saw that guy break up a fight between these two huge bastards with nothing but a cork...

(Pete Jumps onto bar with a cork in his hand – action hero/ dramatic – drum roll / dramatic music))

Pete

Right then, who's arse am I shoving this up? And who's head's going to get it back?

Raymond

Cool.

(Enter Singer – smiles and waves and club members, winks at Ray - sings – 'They're Red Hot by Robert Johnson' – short version)

Hot tamales and they're red hot, yes she got'em for sale
Hot tamales and they're red hot, yes she got'em for sale
I got a girls, say she long and tall
She sleeps in the kitchen with her feets in the hall
Hot tamales and they're red hot, yes she got'em for sale, I mean
Yes, she got'em for sale, yeah Hot tamales and they're red hot,
yes she got'em for sale

Raymond *(Talks over guitar break)*

That's a Robert Johnson number... Robert Johnson... deal with the devil at the crossroads... no? You don't know it. Of all the heads, in all the world... I end up in yours... anyhow it was a great night with great music and I managed to cadge a few drinks too many, I think the last song was Moon River...oh come on! Moon River!

Hot tamales and they're red hot, yes she got'em for sale
She got two for a nickel, got four for a dime
Would sell you more, but they ain't none of mine
Hot tamales and they're red hot, yes she got'em for sale, I mean
Yes, she got'em for sale, yes, yeah Hot tamales and they're red hot,
yes she got'em for sale
Hot tamales and they're red hot, yes she got'em for sale
I got a letter from a girl in the room
Now she got something good she got to bring home soon, now
Its hot tamales and they're red hot, yes she got em for sale, I mean
Yes, she got'em for sale, yeah Hot tamales and they're red hot,
yes she got em for sale

(Raymond starts singing 'drunkenly – the cast join in and then drift from the stage – Raymond is left alone to continue the song – he staggers across the stage. Enter Wendy - they collide.)

Wendy

Where the hell have you been?

Raymond

Shhhh... you'll wake Wendy! Wendy. (Whispers)
I'm home.

Wendy

You're pissed....

Raymond

Beautiful, intelligent, perceptive...and really pissed
off.

Wendy

I don't believe you Ray! I've been worried sick...
did you get the job?

Raymond

Ah... no.

Wendy

No. No? So you decided to get pissed.

Raymond

No... well yes but, I went to the hospital first.

Wendy

Hospital, why did you go to the hospital? What's the matter? What have you done?

Raymond

I collapsed... in a pub. In hindsight I probably shouldn't have mentioned the pub.

Wendy

What were you...? You collapsed in a pub! And then went back for more! What's wrong with you Ray? I can't... you bastard! I don't believe this... I can't deal with this... I'm not stopping here tonight, I'm sick of your... you treat me like dirt, it's not fair Ray, it's not fair! I can't do this anymore...

Raymond

Oh lighten up...

(Wendy slaps him across the face and storms out.)

Raymond

Good point, well made. You see, I was an arse, a
self-pitying drunken arse... but that revelation
didn't truly sink in till later... right now I'm
feeling hard-done-by and hungry....now is the
time for loud music *(Loud music – Tom Waits
'Going Out West – Raymond dances – falls to his
knees)*... chicken...I've got a powerful craving for
chicken! Bring me chicken...I'll do it myself
then...

*(Music stops – Raymond mimes – enter notice
'sandwich board man – S/B Man/ or large cards)*

Side one reads –

"Putting frozen chicken under the grill."

S/B Man then turns, side two reads –

"WARNING! Never cook frozen chicken pissed."

*Raymond mimes checking watch – then mimes
eating chicken.*

Raymond

(To S/B Man) Piss off, I know what I'm doing.
(Exit S/B Man)

You know, I don't think she'll be back tonight...
well sod it...who needs her. A few more bevies
then bed.... More chicken!

(Raymond continues to dance and eat chicken to no music)

(Enter) **S/B Man/Chorus** *(with clipboard)*

Salmonellosis is an infection caused by the Salmonella bacteria. Symptoms include salmon pink diarrhoea, fever, vomiting, and abdominal cramps. Some people believe the condition got its name from the pink salmon coloured diarrhoea, this is a myth. It was discovered in 1885 by Theobald Smith but this infectious shit-storm was eventually named to honour his boss, Daniel Elmer Salmon. Shit Fact number 334.

(Raymond lays on the floor – snores.)

S/B MAN

In severe cases the diarrhoea is so bad that the patient becomes dangerously dehydrated and must be taken to a hospital, where intravenous fluids and antibiotics can be provided...failure to do so, can result in turning into a trout, guppy or, in the worst case scenario, a politician. *(Skips from stage)*

Raymond

Weird dreams… oh the first fart of the day…
(Silent fart - shock) Oh my! *(Stiff legged run off stage)*

Enter S/B Man in 'Bob Dylan' mode – as in Subterranean Homesick Blues film – holding a stack of cards - music in background similar 12bar thrash – cards read

'Death by Chicken - Day 1' -

Raymond (voice off stage)

Oh my God!

'Day 2 – (loud prolonged fart)

Raymond (VoS) Noooo!

Day 3 –

Raymond (VoS) Make it stop, make it stop!

Day 4 –

Raymond (Sings – VoS) Burning ring of fire, oh oh a ring of fire.

(Exit S/B Man/ Dylan – Enter Wendy carrying a suitcase.)

Wendy

Ray! Raymond, where are you!?

(Raymond crawls onto the stage.)

Raymond

Help…

Wendy

I've only come to collect my stuff…

Raymond

I'm ill…

Wendy

I can't help that. We're finished, you know it and I know it… but as usual I've got to be the adult and say it…

Raymond

But now, right now..?

Wendy

I've got to go before I really start hating you...

Raymond

Before you really start? Wendy I love you...

Wendy

Ray... you didn't even notice I'd packed my bags.

Raymond

She wasn't wrong... she gave me that look that
only a broken hearted woman can do...two thirds
pity, one third shame with lots and lots of ice...
sorry baby I've been busy.

Wendy

So have I.

Raymond

Bang, the kill shot. I heard what she said...and I
knew what she meant... I could smell the smoke of
burning bridges, no doubt about it, we were
done... and out the door she went.

(Exit Wendy.)

Raymond

Now as weak and sober as I was…

(Raymond is thrown a rope from off stage-Pulls a funeral pyre of stuffed toys on to stage)

I decided to be grown up about it… and got every piece of tat she'd ever bought me, and burnt the bloody lot in the back yard… that's not common talk, the garden was a yard…. A yard wide and a yard long… not enough room to swing a ladybird really… nice fire though. *(Smoke – drifts across stage.)* Thing is, those cheap stuffed toys, are real fire hazards, and really flammable… *(coughs)* things got a little out of hand (sound of fire engine – flashing lights – stage turns red) My House! Ahhh… my hair! Help!

(Fireman enters and carries Raymond off stage right.)

Raymond

Really not cool!

(Sound or fire engine fade – lights to normal. Enter Dr Caz – stage left. Enter Raymond – stage right - the top of his head is covered in bandages. Dr Caz recognises him, shakes her head and walks off stage past him.)

Raymond

Everything… gone, literally up in smoke… all my records, CD's…even had to accept dead man's clothes from the hospital… *(kneels and rubs the ground)* feel that? … that's rock bottom. And just when you really need an angel…

Beryl (pops up from Behind bar)

Oh my sweaty arse, you look like shit!

Raymond

Class… Real class.

Beryl

So what next Raymond? Got a job? Got anywhere to stay?

Raymond

No job. No home and dead man's clothes… and I seem to have lost a lot of weight.

Beryl

Had a bit of a clear-out ah? You need feeding up boy.

Raymond

Maybe, as long as I never have to see another piece of chicken….

(Beryl places huge KFC bucket on to the bar.)

Beryl

Eat up…

Raymond

Really… I…

Beryl

Eat!

Raymond

Help!

(Raymond tentatively eats chicken – clearly feeling like throwing up with every mouthful.)

Beryl

So here's an idea... I need someone to look after the bar, clean up that kind of thing, I can't pay you much but there's a room upstairs. My brother wants to do it up and let it out. If you help out you can use it till it's done, no rush, give you time to get your thick head together...

Raymond

See that...the woman is a bloody angel.

Beryl

One last thing... you touch the till or the optics and I'll break your bloody fingers... and my brother will eat them!

Raymond

A pretty grim angel for sure but... Sounds like a deal to me. *(Offers his hand-)*

(Beryl comes around the bar, hugs him.)

Beryl

What a wanker!

(And exits – Raymond waves her off grabs KFC bucket and throws up into it)

Raymond

Coleslaw anyone?

(Pete appears from behind bar takes the bucket and hands Raymond duster / bar towel)

Sorry...So cool...

(As Raymond talks the club fills – people chatting, sitting at tables - Raymond is delivering drinks to tables as he talks.)

Believe it or not things actually got better... I got busy and I got better... I didn't touch a drop... didn't even miss it.... But I am thirsty all the time... I drink a lot of water. A lot of water.

Pete

Table two Ray!

Raymond

Weird thing was I could still taste the booze, no
really! That was a lager and lime… and a bitter,
which is a bit off… and if someone spilt a drink…
(Raymond cleans the spill) I could taste it… the
next day… through my feet… probably some
weird ex drinker thing… Watch *(takes off shoe and
feels under table)* Gin and tonic and… ummm …
Babysham?… do people still drink Babysham?
Weird huh? But it was good, it was five weeks of
good.

Beryl

Everybody shut up! Maurice is going to pontificate
as only a pounced up poof can... Pete give the
ponce a Babysham.

Maurice

Why thank you…really too kind. Ray, we know
you've had it tough recently…

Beryl

Mostly his own bloody fault.

Maurice

Distractors to one side… we've had a bit of a collection for you… just to help out. *(Hands Raymond envelope)* Here's to you Ray!

(All cheer)

Beryl

Get some bloody clothes that fit! You look like a wet fart.

Raymond

No believe me I know what a wet fart looks like… I don't know what to say… thank you. Beryl had a point, the one thing I couldn't do was put on weight, in fact I kept losing it. I was using belt, braces and string to keep the strides up!

Pete

Time gentlemen please.

Beryl

Right, come on then, piss off! Pete, just throw the takings in the safe I'll total up in the morning...when I can see straight.

Raymond

I'll nip down to Burtons in the morning... *(Looks into envelope)* or Primart....

Pete

Right you are... night all. See you tomorrow Ray.
(Exits)

Raymond

It had been a great night, too good to end... and for the first time in weeks I felt hungry, so I went in search of some dangerously high cholesterol refreshment... deep fried, battered kebab pizza perhaps...

(Stage Dims - Raymond is walking down a street. Raymond picks up newspaper from the floor)
...and then I noticed the date... it was Wendy's birthday... *(sits on the floor)* which didn't bother me at all... which bothered me... seven years

together and now nothing... what sort of arse was I?

(Enter Wendy holding hands with new fella – she is carrying a bunch of flowers)

Raymond

Uh oh... awkward moment three hundred and forty-five approaching.

(Wendy & New Fella, walk past – and throw some coins at Raymond's feet. Exit)

Raymond

Ouch...

(Two youths run on and give him a kicking.)

Youth

Bloody tramp! *(Exit running)*

Raymond

Double ouch… the night had taken a turn for the
worst…time to call it quits I think… and out
I…go.

*(He collapses into unconsciousness – fade lights.
Black.)*

Act 2

*(Raymond is collapsed centre stage/ music starts -
'The Kinks - You really got me going.' Enter Road
Sweeper with iPod singing same – with great
gusto. He 'sweeps' Raymond's head several times
before Raymond wakes up – and several more
times before he realises Raymond is not a pile of
rubbish.)*

Raymond

Give over! Oi give over! I'm up! I'm up already…

*(Road Sweeper – bows – goes into full 'air guitar
mode' and just carries down the road. Exit stage)*

Raymond

That might have been allegorical? New broom
time for Raymond?…I think not…I knew
something was wrong as soon as I got back to the
club …apart from tasting Babysham through my
shoes, there was something else… something cold
and metallic, like sour copper…what is that?

(Raymond picks up a paper bag from the bar.)
Chicken sandwiches and Pepto Bismal… Beryl,
you here? *(Picks up cigarette)*… what is that taste?
Beryl! *(He moves to go behind the bar and freezes)*
Beryl…oh my God Beryl.

*(Unseen - Beryl's murdered body – lights dim –
Raymond nearly vomits – visibly shaken moves to
front of stage. Police lights / sirens. Enter Police
officers – and photographer)*

Raymond

I'd never seen so much blood…

Police Inspector

And you didn't hear anybody come into the
premises Mr Ekal? Not even…

Raymond

I was out all night…she shouldn't have been here,
it was too early, she's never in this early.

Police Inspector

So why do you think she was here?

Raymond

I think she brought me those sandwiches
… I've been ill.

Police Inspector

And did you go into the back office?

Raymond

Only to use the phone…

Police Inspector

You didn't notice anything untoward in the office?

Raymond

The safe's been forced…

Police Inspector

You'll have to go down to the station and make a statement Mr Ekal, clear up a few loose ends…

Police Officer

Inspector! *(Officer holds up a bloody crowbar)*

Police Inspector

Bag it… that will be all for now Mr Ekal.

(Lights dim – spot light on Raymond)

Raymond

Turns out they found an unknown set of prints on the crowbar, I was out of the loop. Whoever they were they wanted the night's takings. On my reckoning, there was four hundred and fifty quid in the safe… what's the world coming to ah? The wake was an event….

(Enter the mourners – with much laughter and chat – blues music)

Big Bob

She was my big sister, she looked after me when I
was nothing but a snot nosed kid, my fucking role
model she was… one of a kind…To Beryl!

All

To Beryl

Maurice

Let's hope they haven't enforced the smoking ban
beyond the pearly gates yet… or banned spitting or
swearing…

Big Bob

Hello, you're the geezer found my sister.

Raymond

I am

Big Bob

She liked you. She told me so. You've been
staying in the flat above the club right? The thing
is Ray…I've got plans for that room.

Raymond

I see…When do you want me out?

Big Bob

Very decent of you Ray, look no rush, no rush;
give it till the end of the month.

Raymond

Which is in two weeks.

Big Bob

Maybe you could help me out with something else
Ray? The club was Beryl's baby, not really my cup
of tea, not got time for it either.

Raymond

You want me to look after the club? No problem.

Big Bob

Good man. Just till the end of the month… then
I'm closing it, gonna put in some flats. Beryl never
appreciated what a nice little earner she was sitting
on.

Raymond

A thought occurred to me, probably the same one you're having now… maybe Big Bob bumped off his own sister? *(Bob hugs Raymond)* Now this is the weird thing… firstly, he smells just like you'd think and… I could feel his sweat….I could taste it through my skin… I could hear his thoughts in my head…

Big Bob *(to audience – turns into mewling babe)*

I loved my sister! When I find the bastard who did this I'm gonna feed him through a meat grinder feet first…slowly! And then I'll turn into sausages and feed them to his kids… or his parents…or his dog…and if he aint got a dog… I'll buy him a dog and let him keep it long enough to love it and then… *(tears).*

Raymond

Guess it wasn't him then.

Big Bob *(Hugs Ray again)*

Nice fella… for a queer. Take care Ray, take care. *(Exits)*

Raymond

He's going to shut the club... his sister's ashes
aren't even cold yet and he's closing her club...
what an arsehole. But to be honest...that whole
mind reading bit had got my attention... I needed
to get some air...

*(Enter busy 'going to work' people – stage left
and stage right. Sound of thunder. Busy people
start putting up umbrellas, collars, sheltering
under newspapers – then they freeze in mid action)*

Raymond

I thought I was going mad... I could see the rain.
A thousand rain drops stopped in mid-air, right in
front of me, all around me! I looked up and the sky
was full of shimmering shards of glass.

Busy P 1

Bloody Rain

Busy P 2

These shoes are killing me!

Busy P 3

Ummm nipples...

Busy P 2

I knew I should have worn those boots

Raymond

Those weren't my thoughts! They weren't even in my voice, but they were in my head. I could hear them reverberating inside, talking over one another, cramming into my head. There was only one explanation – I'd flipped my lid, and that's a truly terrifying thought.

(The Busy People start moving – Busy P 2 (female) stops next to Raymond.)

Busy P 2

Did I turn off the iron?

Raymond

I could hear her thinking... where is it? *(Busy P 2 looks through handbag)* Where is it? I know I put it in here...aha!

Busy P 2

(Into mobile) Hi Joe, did I turn the iron off? I did, right okay. Anything we need? No there's bread in the freezer, that's the fridge Joe...oh never mind. Men.

Raymond

It was the same voice... I heard inside my head *(SHOUTS)* what the hell is going on here!?

(Busy P – stop and stare at him)

All Busy P

Bloody Drunk!

(Raymond's trousers fall down – Exit Busy People. Raymond puts on dressing gown –it is now huge and he is diminished by it)

Raymond

That is not normal... clothes don't stretch in the rain... except maybe wool ... *(Checks label in trousers)* Man made... and what about this? *(Takes off shoe)* Look! I'm a size ten, been a ten for years, these are a ten... but they don't fit anymore... I'm shrinking! How can that be happening? Unless? I

need a pencil! *(Takes pencil out of pocket.)*
Handy.

(Runs to the side wall and marks off his height.)
So... you see either I'm so crazy I don't know I'm
crazy or...or the world's gone crazy and that's
crazy! People don't shrink ...so I must be crazy.

(Runs off to wall and measures himself again)
Laughs...it's okay... I am crazy... unless...

*(Goes behind bar – produces a pint of water – he
splashes a few drops on his face)* Bugger... he
pours it over his head... why did I use the cold
tap? Okay...

*(Measures self against wall – double checks –
returns slowly to centre stage. Sits.)*

Chorus (Now German voice.)

The subject seems to be shrinking. Not possible...
impossible, people don't shrink, jumpers shrink,
not people, and he is people not jumper!

Raymond

Of course, I know...I need to drink, all I need to
do is replace the fluid... *(Looks at the pint glass –
runs back to bar – another full pint which he
downs)*

Chorus

A good idea da, but of course what goes in must
come out, which the subject is now discovering…
with the overpowering need to, as you say,
spending the penny.

Raymond

*(Raymond back to audience – pees into pint glass
– he falls over.)* Oh bugger!! *(Uses dressing gown
to clean up) Look at me, now I'm covered
in…penny! (He goes back to measure line – he's
shrunk again)*

Chorus

Ugh the dirty little swine! He has discovered the
more he drinks…

Raymond

The more I pee. I'm going to…

Chorus

Penny your life away… nothing new there then…
domcoff *(Exit)*

(Enter Pete - appears behind bar)

Raymond

Pete! The coolest guy on the planet! If anybody
will know what to do, it will be Pete... Pete... can
I talk to you...

Pete

Sure, why not... what's up?

Raymond

So cool! Pete I've been... since my accident...
I've been going through some changes... seeing
things...differently and... I think I'm...

Pete

Ray, I'm really touched you decided to tell me first
mate, but no-one's going to be surprised, we've
just been waiting for you to come out... let's be
clear you're not my type but if you need some
introductions or showing around the scene, I'm
more than happy to help out... well done mate, be
loud be proud be queer! (Exit)

Raymond

Mad, shrinking and I give off a gay vibe... and
Pete doesn't fancy me! I'm going out ... lot to
think about... I may be sometime.

*(Lights flicker - Sound of underground train –
enter Busy People – they crowd around Raymond.)*

British Rail Announcer (VoS)

"Mind the gap!"

Raymond

Rush hour... don't you just love rush hour... no
me neither.

BP 3

Look at the arse on that! What I wouldn't give
to...

Raymond

Uh oh...

BP 1

I'm gonna get home and cover me-self with
custard and wait till he comes home.

Raymond

Why is this happening?

BP 4

It's so hot in here.

Raymond

Yes it is…good point…

BP 3

God he stinks. Buy some soap! Disgusting!

Raymond

Sweat… it's their sweat… water

Raymond

Their thoughts, their feelings, hungers and
sensations… I can't keep them out!

Busy People – rapidly then together.

BP 1– Lovely big tits you could ….brrrrbrrrr.

BP 2 – God he stinks, haven't you ever heard of
soap.

BP 3 – A finger of fudge is just enough to give
your kids a treat, a finger of fudge is just enough
until it's time to eat…

BP 4 – Where did I put that umbrella?

(Their voices – merge into a 'train' rhythm)

I wanna get home I wanna get home I wanna get
home

Raymond

Could be worse I guess…

BP 4 (Taps iPod)

Why isn't this playing?

(The Cast line dance and sing song – while Raymond begs for mercy!)

(* Originally I imagined the cast singing and line dancing to R.E.M's 'Shiny Happy People' – however the song may be too good – some up to date crass pop song that Ekal would hate is best here. Raymond also sings along but also calls out for "Help" at appropriate points.)

The train stops "Mind the Gap" - Busy People get off. Raymond remains silent, still.

Raymond

That was horrible…I spent the night by the river. Clearly, I was as crazy as a box of frogs but it felt so… alive!

(Silence)

I need a hospital… but which kind? Tropical diseases, mad house, Hospital of Bloody Impossible Diseases… I wandered around for most of the night and then popped into a greasy spoon café… and there she was…

(Enter Dr Caz – she sits at a table, sipping coffee and reading a text book. Raymond sits at another table – Enter waiter who places a coffee in front of Raymond and then leans against the bar watching Raymond.

Raymond

Just when you need a doctor…along comes one with enough puss filled attitude to infect the whole of known world… still… she was also my only chance…of course what I wanted her to say is…

Dr Caz

My god you're a medical marvel, together we'll rewrite the text books, I shall devote my life to saving you… but first wouldn't you like to examine my…

Raymond

Well I'm still a man….You get the picture. Of course I knew it wasn't going to go that way… she's leaving.

(Dr Caz gets up leaves a tip and walks across stage – to front stage left – Raymond runs to her table and picks up her coffee cup – then follows- the waiter moves to back stage right.)

Raymond

Excuse me…sorry… you won't remember me but… you saved my life.

Dr Caz

I did.

Raymond

Well you gave me some very good advice... about drinking.

Dr Caz

Oh yes, I think I do remember... you've lost weight.

Raymond

Yes... well I stopped drinking, then I got food poisoning.

Dr Caz

I was probably harsher with you than I should have been, apparently I do that a lot.

Raymond

No, I needed to hear it. I want to thank you.

Dr Caz

That's very sweet of you?

Raymond

The thing is, I keep losing weight and... I'm shrinking. I'm three inches shorter than I was four weeks ago. And what's more... I can hear people's thoughts.

Dr Caz

I think you need a different kind of doctor, go and see your GP.

Raymond

I know it sounds crazy but I...Wait I can prove it. *(He licks the cup)* You think your boyfriends a jerk and he doesn't appreciate you.

Dr Caz

Wow...magic.

Raymond

Wait please, I'm not kidding you. *(Licks cup)*
You're wondering why you can't find a decent
bloke who appreciates you for who you are and
won't tie you down. You think your boyfriend's
irresponsible and over powering... hold on a
minute, what is it with you women? Do you even
listen to yourselves? You don't want a man you
want a poodle!

*(Dr Caz produces a can of L'Oreal hairspray from
her bag.)*

Dr Caz

Go away. Don't make me use this?

Raymond

What are you going to do? Backcomb me to death.

Dr Caz

Go away.

Raymond

Look, I'm not going to hurt you. I need your help, I'm shrinking and I can read people thoughts! It happens if I touch something I can... *(He steps forward – she sprays him – he falls to the floor screaming.)*

Dr Caz

I'm sorry...please get some help. (Exit)

(The waiter rushes snatches the cup from Ray and then puts the boot in.)

Waiter

Don't steal my cups. You are a very creepy man... I don't like you. *(Exits)*

(Raymond slowly lifts himself from the floor and eases himself into a chair. Pete appears behind the bar - he pours drinks, sets it down before Ray and sits next to him.)

Raymond

So...cool.

(Maurice joins them)

Pete

This is my last night boys, I've got a gig down at
the Kings Head.

Raymond

Isn't that a gay bar?

Maurice

With a name like that…of course.

Pete

I had you tagged wrong didn't I Ray?

Raymond

Fraid so…sorry…I'm sure it's my fault.

Maurice

What you thought he was…? Peter darling…
really your gaydar was well off there.

Pete

It's never been wrong before…

Maurice

Nonsense, I mean for god's sake some people have
me down as queer. And there's nothing I like more
than giving my wife a damn good rogering.

(Pause)

Raymond

Truth is Pete, I have no idea what I am any more
or what I'm becoming.

Pete

Life's a weird journey…

Maurice

Full of twists and turns, falls and slips…but the
secret is…

Raymond

If you say get up again...I'll break your spine.

Maurice

You know what happens if you stay in the gutter
Ray...you get washed down the drain.

Raymond

True...very true, sorry Maurice, feeling a bit... do
you think they'll ever find Beryl's killer?

Pete

Who can say?

Maurice

I would have thought we'd have heard by now but
these things can take years...

Pete

Would we know if Big Bob had... sorted it?

Maurice

Oh god yes, that thug would put an announcement in The Sun.

Raymond

I think Maurice is right, if they were going to catch him... they would have done it by now...

Maurice

To Beryl and justice...

Raymond

Where ever they may be...

(They clink glasses and Pete returns to the bar)

Pete

Bloody hell...listen to that rain, bucketing it down. We're in for a real storm. *(Exits)*

Maurice

We all miss Beryl darling ... Mustn't miss my
tube, take care of yourself Ray. *(Exits)*

(lights dim – spot light on Raymond)

Raymond

*(Goes up to measuring post and finds he has
shrunk more – he laughs)*

Wasting away... wasted, totally wasted. To quote
a song... *(Enter)*

Chorus

Is it better to burn out than to fade away? To be or
not to be that is the question, it is a far, far better
thing I do now than I have ever done, it is life and
life only, it's all right Ma I'm only bleedin', it is a
far far better place, if you feel like giving up...
hold on, hold on don't let yourself go... or by
opposing... end them, don't get angry get even!
Seek and destroy! I wanna be, anarchy! *(Exit)*

Raymond

I've never done anything good... never seen a good outcome because I was there... and now I'm wasting away...turning into a glass of water... ...what if let the rain wash away all my troubles away... let it wash me away... to be or... to be another... I wasn't going to be missed....I went to the roof...

(Darkness - Thin blue spot light on a 'cruxified' Raymond)

Blues Singer (Enter far left – sings)

I was in the rain, I was the rain, I am the streams, the sea and the rain again, in and out of the world and people, trees and grass, almost disappearing, free at last, free at last... one and many, the whole world over and over, thinner than a raindrop, deeper than the oceans... I was the rain, I was the rain, I am the rain... *(Exits)*

(Raymond centre stage – in a hunched ball - Sound of a raised heart beat – Raymond kneeling in spot light.)

Raymond

Drains and pipes and pipes and drains and lakes
and seas and rain again to fall into pipes and
drains...And then... here I am... inside your
head... and you know why I'm here don't you... it
took a long time, you weren't easy to find... but
here we are... you should have listened... never
drink the water...too late for begging...you
shouldn't have hurt my friend... I wonder what
damage I could do now that I'm here between your
synapses... what could I make you see what could
I make you do...

*(Enter Beryl – covered in blood – stands beside
Raymond – starts coughing)*

See what you have done... see what I can do...

*(Enter Cast – stand around Raymond in semicircle
– they start to cough – randomly, out of sequence)*

Oh the fun we shall have now that I'm here to stay
(Coughs) I'm here to make you pay...

*(Coughing gets louder, louder continuous – heart
beat louder – Raymond screams in rage and
victory)*

Raymond

Now that I'm here...I'm really going to fuck you
up.

(Lights out – the sound of a dripping tap –
growing louder and louder - silence.)

END

Authors Note

Birthing Drip or iDRIP as it became had a long and convoluted process, but the initial idea was simple enough; whats the strangest story I could write?

Originally a film script that became an interactive novel – with clues about Raymond's demise hidden on the internet – told from the point of view of D.I Sims and Ray's found diary. The piece focused on the cult of the ever living Raymond Ekal – it was however hampered by two significant issues - firstly it was poorly written and then its ending had to make sense – even in the entire concept was fantastical the end had to fit that world…and the ending I had, didn't work.

It took somewhere between sixteen and eighteen years – and many, many rewrites - to finally stumble upon the solution and in so doing the novel became a short story (available via Weasel Press – Tales in Liquid Time). But this wouldn't have been achieved if I hadn't broken away from the literary format and gone back to the idea of a script, although this time intended for the stage, and it is for this reason that iDRIP The Play is presented here.

Although its staging as I envisioned it clearly owes much to Brecht, I'm sure younger and more technologically aware eyes could see other possibilities that have escaped me, however as the theatre audience is required to be the silent and unwitting character within the play I saw such Brechtian tropes as not only unavoidable but downright essential and therefore make no apology for using a style which is as often in vogue as it is dated.

The core story, as I see it, is that of redemption by suffering and vengeance by force of will – it matters not if Raymond is mad or if his story is true – all that matters is that he embraces his fate and uses it to set right a wrong…but that is just my opinion…which may change…as for its telling and staging I regard that as fluid as Raymond.

The script was intended to be used and useful, it is not written on stone but in water so as to an adaptable piece for small to middling to larger theatre companies…so have fun with it.

Yours

N S. Reddy 2016

NB – Ekal Backwards?

DANK HOUSE MANOR PUBLISHING

Hearts on a Barbed Wire Fence

by

J. E Badham

Interzone Xpress Boogie

By

Neil S. Reddy

Reginald Robin Bastard

by

Ian Parker

www.ingramcontent.com/pod-product-compliance
Lightning Source LLC
Chambersburg PA
CBHW060534030426
42337CB00021B/4257